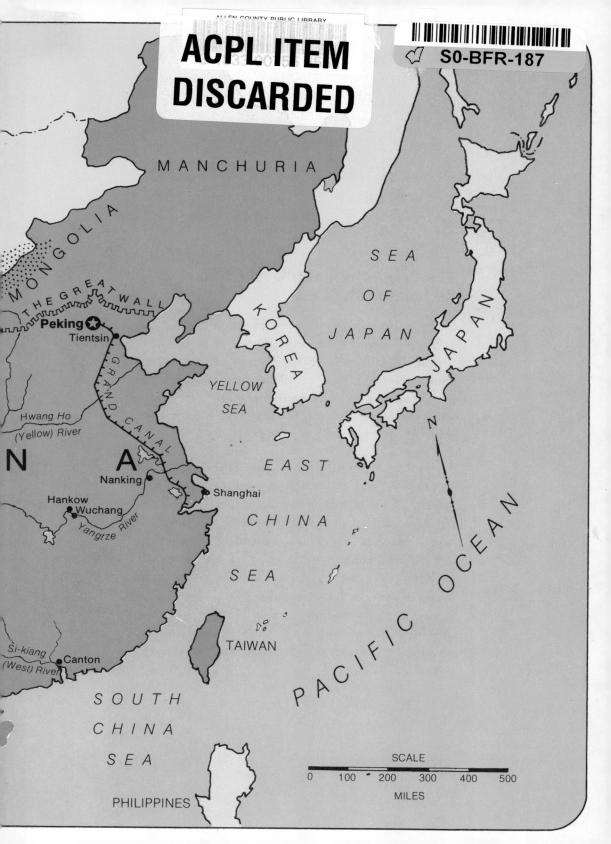

MANCHURIA

MONGOLIA

THE GREAT WALL

Peking ⭐
Tientsin

KOREA

SEA

OF

JAPAN

JAPAN

GRAND CANAL

Hwang Ho
(Yellow) River

YELLOW

SEA

N

A

Nanking

Hankow
Wuchang

Yangtze River

Shanghai

EAST

CHINA

SEA

N

CHINA

Si-kiang
(West) River

Canton

TAIWAN

PACIFIC OCEAN

SOUTH

CHINA

SEA

PHILIPPINES

SCALE

0   100   200   300   400   500

MILES

The People's Republic of China:
Red Star of the East

offers a rare firsthand view of mainland China,
home to more than one-quarter of the earth's
people. The borders of this ancient country, which
were closed to most outsiders for more than a
generation, are opened here to reveal a new China
where traditional ways of living have undergone a
dramatic change.

To explain more fully the origin of the Communist
Revolution and the sweeping reforms that have
taken place in the generation since, the stories and
legends found in other books in this series have
been omitted. Emphasis instead is placed on
helping the young reader to obtain a better understanding of the geography, history, and ways of
living of this Far Eastern nation. The effects of the
Communist Revolution on people's lives at home,
in school, and at work are reported as they were observed by the author on a recent visit to the People's
Republic of China.

THE PEOPLE'S REPUBLIC OF
CHINA
RED STAR OF THE EAST

By JANE WERNER WATSON

GARRARD PUBLISHING COMPANY
CHAMPAIGN, ILLINOIS

Library of Congress Cataloging in Publication Data

Watson, Jane Werner, 1915-
    The People's Republic of China.

    Includes index.
    SUMMARY: A geographic, historic, and social survey
of the People's Republic of China.

    1. China—Juvenile literature. [1. China]
I. Title.
DS706.W335   951.05   75-42275
ISBN 0-8116-6863-0

Photo credits:

The Bettmann Archive: pp. 27, 31, 49, 59
Brown Brothers: p. 54
Freer Gallery of Art, Smithsonian Institution: p. 23
Georg Gerster/Rapho/Photo Researchers: pp. 4, 18
Paolo Koch/Rapho/Photo Researchers: pp. 1, 43, 67, 78, 85, 88, 94, 102, 106
Michael J. O'Neill/*The New York News:* pp. 3, 7, 71, 83, 91, 104
Audrey Topping/Rapho/Photo Researchers: pp. 13, 34, 75, 81
Jane Werner Watson: cover
Wide World Photos: p. 38

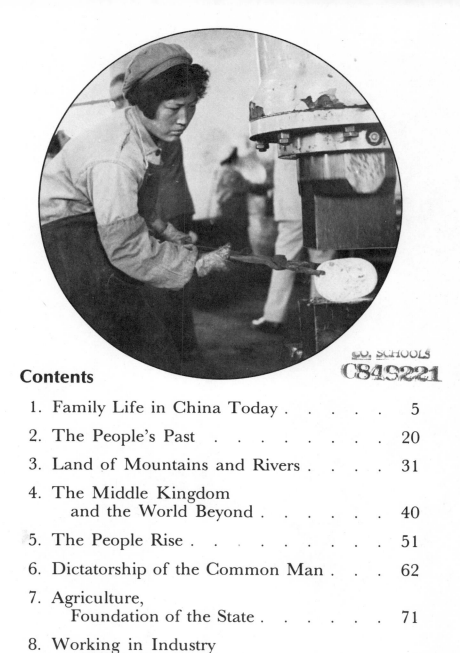

Contents

Throngs of pedestrians share a busy street in Peking
with wagons, buses, and bicycle riders.

1. Family Life in China Today

It is noontime. The city streets are full of life and noise. Bus drivers honk their horns at bicyclists. Men on bicycles push their tinkling bells to warn those on foot. The sidewalks are so crowded with people that many walk in the streets. In fact, a lane has been marked off on some city streets for pedestrians. Where are people going in such crowds and in such a hurry? Home for their noonday meal.

Of course not everyone is on his way home. Some are headed for department stores or small shops. And some will stop to eat at snack shops along the streets. Tables in these shops are crowded with people bent over bowls of rice or noodles. Other customers are waiting for steaming hot dumplings stuffed with vegetables or meat. Some workers also eat in their factory cafeterias. But most people in China like to go home for the midday meal.

School children go home even if their parents work too far away to make the round trip at noon. Usually there is a grandparent at home to prepare the meal. If not, some friendly neighbor woman who no longer goes out to work sees that the children are well fed.

Children too young for school may spend their days in a nursery at the factory where their mothers work. Even if a mother works nights, the factory nursery is open. Babies as young as eight weeks of age may be taken there. Then the new mother goes back to her job. The mother has time off from work to feed her baby in the nursery.

At mealtime each child in the nursery who is old enough carries a small painted wooden chair to one of the low tables. The helpers bring out from the small, steamy kitchen plates of hot lunch. One day the lunch may be egg drops, pork cut in bite-size bits, and cooked spinach hearts.

At a factory day nursery, a group of young dancers entertains the smaller children.

After lunch the children nap. And at the end of the work day, their mothers pick them up and take them home.

Home in the City

Workshops for women have been included in the new workers' residential areas. So the mother usually works close to home. The father of the family, however, may bicycle across town to his factory or office.

There is not much need for mothers of young children to stay home all day. Most families, particularly in cities, do not have more than two children. "One is fine," posters say, "two is all right, three is too many." Day nursery care is available for all small children. And there is not a great deal of housework for the mother to do.

Homes are small. Most families have two rooms and a kitchen that they may share with one or two other families. The modern apartment buildings in workers' areas are usually not more than three stories tall, though some in large cities have four or five floors. An outside door and stairway lead to three or four apartment doors on each floor.

In the family's apartment each of the two rooms usually holds a double bed. A low bed for a child can be slid under one of these during the day. This is often necessary because most families include four or five people. There may be grandparents, a mother and father, and one small child. Or perhaps there are parents and two children.

In the larger of the two rooms, along with the bed there is a square table for meals, with chairs and stools enough for the family. Most homes have a sewing machine and a radio. And there is storage space for extra clothing, usually in a chest or a tall wardrobe.

People take pride in their homes. Most of these homes are more comfortable than those the families lived in before the Communist takeover of China in 1949.

"Before liberation," says one worker, "I supported my parents although I was only a boy." "Liberation" is the word most people use for the start of the Communist era. They speak of the time before as "the bitter past." "In the bitter past six of us slept on the cold floor in one room. Now we have all this." The worker waves at his bright, pleasant room. "We have a happy life, thanks to Chairman Mao."

Chairman Mao was the first leader of the Chinese Communist government. Hundreds of millions of people still think of him as a father and guide.

Under the Communist government rents are very low, about five percent of the family's income. Electricity costs very little. Food takes a sizable share of the income, but the government keeps prices from rising.

Health care is very, very inexpensive. There is a clinic in every city neighborhood and in every rural community or commune. If the clinic does not have a fully trained doctor, at least it has a nurse and a paramedic, or "barefoot doctor." They make house calls, take care of simple ailments, and know when someone should be sent to a hospital.

No one needs to worry about not being taken care of in old age. Men generally retire from work at the age of 60 and women at 55. After that they are paid 70 percent of their last salary. And they find plenty to do in their neighborhoods.

Some serve on the committees that run the neighborhood or village. These are called revolutionary committees. Others conduct after-school study groups for young people. Or they help slow learners. There are neighborhood centers where people can join groups for sports or hobbies. And there are usually some neighbors who need help. They may be old or sick and have no family. If so, someone will stop in to visit and fix their meals. Caring about others is important.

Old-Style Homes

Many people live in homes that were built long before the days of Communism. Most of these are one-story houses with walls of stone, brick, or whitewashed mud. Lumber has been scarce in China for a long time, so wooden walls or ornaments have been considered a sign of wealth. Roofs are of red or gray tiles or, in the country, often of thatch.

Rural families may still own their small houses. Farmland now belongs to the community, since the Communists do not believe in private ownership. But many farm workers have been permitted to keep their homes. These do not usually have more than two rooms.

A big clay platform called a *kang* often occupies a good deal of the space. It has an oven below. Most of the family sleeps on the warm, flat top. They sleep on grass mats with padded cotton quilts that are folded up during the day. Cooking is done on a small stove which is often built into a corner of the room. There is not much furniture.

In the old days the homes of rich landowners and city businessmen were very large. But these men had large families to house. Grandparents lived surrounded by their married sons with wives and children, all under the same set of roofs. Each subfamily had its own rooms.

Looking at one of these old-fashioned Chinese homes from the outside, all one sees is a long low wall with upturned tile eaves curling above it at the corners. This wall may stretch along a narrow paved lane in a large city, or it may be out in the open countryside.

At the center of the wall is the main gateway to the house, roofed with a small peaked hat of tile. Looking in at the gateway, one cannot see much. A flat panel called a spirit screen blocks the view.

People used to believe that evil spirits could not turn corners. If the spirits could not enter a house in a straight line, they could not harm the people inside. So spirit screens were set up across doorways to keep bad spirits out. Even factories often have these screens inside their gates. Today the screens are painted with political slogans such as, "Go all out, aim high, and achieve greater results in building socialism."

Beyond the spirit screen of an old home lies an open courtyard with rooms opening onto it. Often a second courtyard lies beyond some of the rooms.

Today these large old homes are divided into a great many small apartments, since there are no longer any rich families in China. The former owner of a big home may still live in it. But probably he will have just two rooms, like any other tenant.

A Day at Home

Early to bed and early to rise is the rule in most Chinese homes. In the farming villages or rural communes, families get up about five in the morning, especially during the growing season. The parents and older children work in the fields or in the family garden plot for a couple of hours before breakfast. In town, grown-ups often join their friends outside on the street for early morning exercises while radio loudspeakers blare lively music.

Young people draw the day's supply of water at a rural commune in Manchuria.

Since many homes do not have running water, often someone has to go to the well to fill the big water jars. Bathing is done with water in an enamel wash basin since there are few bathtubs. A big kettle of water is kept hot on the stove most of the time.

Breakfast is eaten about seven o'clock. Usually it includes some sort of rolls or biscuits and a salted or pickled vegetable with noodles—in the north of China—or thin rice soup.

Then children go off to school and parents to work. On rural communes work teams march to the fields with red banners waving above them.

Both students and workers have a break during the morning. And there is generally a long lunch hour, so that most people can get home for the noonday meal.

A couple of times a week the parents are expected to attend meetings, perhaps during the noon hour. At these meetings politics is discussed, especially the teachings of Mao Tse-tung and other Communist leaders. And people criticize anyone who, they feel, has not been doing his share of work.

The school day ends for young people long before their parents' work day is over. But grandparents and "aunties and uncles" in the neighborhood hold study groups in some of their homes to make certain that the children do their homework.

Much of the housekeeping is done by grandmothers. Girls in the family may help them sweep the floors and doorways and throw the wash water outside the door to keep down the dust.

A tree branch with its twigs broken short to form hooks hangs beside many front doors. Everyone coming into the house hangs his shoes on one of these hooks, to keep from muddying the floor.

An important part of the housekeeping is cooking. In the south of China the most basic food is rice; in the north, noodles. Beans, squash, cabbage, cucumbers, and greens are eaten on the rice or noodles, sometimes with bits of pork or fish. There is often soup, too, perhaps with noodles or egg drop or squares of soy bean curd afloat in it. Bread is made of wheat or corn flour and is usually steamed. This makes it moist and gives it a soft texture.

Parents or grandparents often feed small children by hand until they are four or five years old. Teachers and helpers in nursery schools and kindergartens say they have to feed some new children for a few days, to keep them from being homesick. But soon they are handling chopsticks neatly for themselves.

Older children often like to take their rice bowls and chopsticks to the window or doorway of their home, so they can watch what is going on outside as they eat.

Free Time

Work days in factories are eight hours long. For those who work on farms they are longer. Sometimes grown-ups have to go out at night to open or close irrigation channels or to cover plants when there is danger of frost. Of course some city people work at night, too, in busy factories.

Everyone, including school children, works six days a week. The free day of the week is not the same for everyone. Schools are closed on Sundays, but factory workers have different days off. The mother and father in a family may not be free on the same day. Everyone has some day off each week, though. And there is plenty to do on it.

Many men like to play cards or Chinese chess with their friends on a sunny doorstep or sidewalk. Others like to sit quietly on a river-bank and fish by the hour. Groups may gather at a snack shop or at a workers' cultural center for a chat or an adult education course. Women may join group activities too. Or they may take their knitting or sewing out into the sunshine where neighbors pass by.

Boys and girls like to play games and visit with their friends in their free time. In the summer they like to swim. In the winter they may slide or skate on frozen ponds or streams. If they show special talent in some direction, they may be selected for training in dancing, music, sports, or gymnastics at a Children's Palace or at one of the Sparetime Physical Training Schools.

School children have weeks free in the winter and in the summer. But grown-ups have no paid vacations. When a holiday gives everyone in the family a free day at the same time, then it is a good time to plan a special excursion. The family may take a picnic to a park. They may go to the movies or an opera. These tell stories about the importance of working for Communism and the state. Or the family may visit one of the old mansions, palaces, and temples that are now open to the public.

At Peking's Summer Palace, working people come to see the places where noblemen once strolled.

The most famous and most visited is the huge palace compound in Peking where the families of many emperors lived. When emperors ruled China these vast palaces were known as the Forbidden City. Common people were never permitted to enter. Now they belong to all the people, and families like to visit them. They admire the carved marble dragons, the gilded lions, the sunny courtyards. They marvel at the beautiful throne rooms under their upcurled tile roofs. And they walk slowly through rooms filled with treasures of porcelain, jade, gold, and jewels.

18

Many other palaces, old temples with stately statues, and pagodas whose roofs rise like tall stacks of tile hats are open to the public. There are gardens to be visited too. These were made hundreds of years ago for emperors or wealthy nobles. They are filled with graceful small pavilions and pools of water that mirror humpbacked bridges. One steps carefully over the sills of moon-shaped gateways and finds stiff old armchairs still arranged for tea in some open-sided pavilion. The chairs face, across a mirrored pool, a small painted stage. Dancers used to twirl and pose gracefully there, while musicians played haunting tunes, but only for the garden's owner and his honored guests.

Today workers, peasants, soldiers, and their families stroll through these beautiful spots and marvel at the lovely things made by their forefathers long, long ago. The people of China work hard today to build a better future. But they never forget their country's long, proud, and sometimes bitter past.

2. The People's Past

In the north of China the Hwang Ho, or Yellow River, tumbles down from the western mountains. It flows across a broad plain eastward to the Yellow Sea. It was in this river valley that the first Chinese villages and towns grew up, thousands of years ago.

Those villagers, who called themselves the Black-haired People, did not have an easy life. Winters were cold, as they still are in north China. Icy winds blew down through the mountain passes.

When spring melted the ice in the rivers and the snow on the high mountains, flood waters often swept across fields and through homes. And summers were so hot and dry that many crops wilted for lack of water.

The Black-haired People learned to live with this harsh climate. They built homes of sun-baked mud for shelter against the cold. They constructed dikes along the river banks to hold in flood waters. They dug canals to carry water to their crops during the hot summers.

To build these projects and then keep them in working order, the people had to learn to work together. This took rules. These rules for working and living together were the beginning of government.

Leaders saw to it that each household contributed its share of work or goods. Gradually each farmer began to pay part of his crops to the leader as a tax. When crops were good, a leader could become rich. Then he could pay more people to work for him.

The more taxes a leader collected, the more powerful he became. Some of the leaders even had their own armies with which they took over nearby villages. These leaders were called warlords. Some of them controlled so much territory that they were like kings.

Warlords have been important all through the history of China. Most of the families of kings or emperors came to power by being strong and clever warriors. When a warlord became so powerful that he took over the throne, people said he "had a mandate (a command) from Heaven." So emperors came to be called "Sons of Heaven."

A family of kings who pass on the rule to their heirs is called a dynasty. One of the earliest of these, the Shang dynasty, came to power more than 3,500 years ago. The last royal family, the Manchu or Ch'ing dynasty, lost the throne only in 1911.

As a "Son of Heaven" the emperor had certain sacred duties to the people. At planting season and certain other times, he went onto the land. There he made offerings to the spirits of the mountains and rivers, to the land, the sun, and heaven. The people believed that these spirits controlled their lives and fortunes. The ceremonies were supposed to make the crops grow well and to keep the country prosperous. Between the special ceremonies, the emperors and other members of the royal families had little to do with their people.

In addition to farming, in the valleys of the Yellow River and of the Yangtze farther south, people were developing many other skills. They learned to melt certain rocks in hot fires to make metals—first bronze, then iron. Metal

These hollow bronze tigers were cast in China over 2,000 years ago.

tools helped farmers and builders and other craftsmen to do better work. Some of these people learned to shape bronze with such skill that we marvel today at the beauty of their three-footed cooking pots and water or wine jugs decorated with fanciful animal forms.

Most of the beautiful things these artist-craftsmen made went to the palaces of the kings and the homes of wealthy nobles. When these people died, many lovely objects of jade, bronze, lacquered wood, and silk were buried with them for their use—it was believed—in an afterlife.

Not one of the ancient palaces remains to be seen today. But occasionally one of the old tombs is uncovered. The objects in it show us a good deal about how the wealthy and powerful lived long ago. The tomb furnishings and ornaments also tell us how many talented and skillful workers there must have been among the common folk, to make all those fine objects. To the people of China today the accomplishments of workers of the past are most important. But long ago these skillful workers were little appreciated by the rich and powerful.

The Silk Road

One of the great discoveries of the early Chinese was the spinning and weaving of silk. Legend says that it was the fourteen-year-old bride of an early emperor—perhaps about 2700 B.C.!—who first unwound the delicate strands of a silkworm cocoon.

Before very long many workers were kept busy collecting silkworm cocoons from the leaves of mulberry trees, boiling the cocoons, and then unwinding the raw silk. These finer-than-hair fibers were twisted into thread and woven into beautiful cloth.

For many hundreds of years, it was only in

24

China that the secret of silk-making was known. Camel and pony caravans carried bolts of silk across deserts and over snowy mountain passes to the West.

Ancient Romans were willing to pay its weight in gold for silk. Mighty Persians of 2,500 years ago bought bolts of cloth, then ordered servants to unravel all the woven threads and to reweave them in Persian designs. But no one could discover the source of this glowing and beautiful thread.

It was in the year 550 that two Christian monks on a visit to China discovered how the silk was made. They hid some silkworm eggs and mulberry seeds in their walking sticks and carried them back to their emperor in Constantinople. From then on silkworms fed on mulberry leaves were raised in the West. Silk was soon being woven there. But Chinese silks have continued to be highly valued all over the world to this very day.

Writing and Other Arts

The Chinese people also led the world in the making of paper. In ancient Egypt, sheets of papyrus reed had for many years been cut and flattened out for writing. But these sheets were necessarily small. They had to be pasted together to make a long scroll.

It was about 1,900 years ago when someone in China learned how to boil tree bark or rags to a pulp, then spread a thin layer of this pulp out on a smooth surface to dry. Thus a sheet of paper of any size could be made.

Soon Chinese artists were drawing on paper. Long before they had paper on which to work, they had painted on the plaster walls of temples, palaces, and tombs. They had drawn and painted on strips of silk and on clay pots. And for about 2,000 years the Chinese have been painting on vases, jars, and figurines of porcelain.

Porcelain, like silk, was made only in China for almost 1,800 years. During all those years nowhere else had people found the special pure-white, soft clay called kaolin. Nowhere else had they learned to mix their clay with a special kind of ground stone to make very hard, gleaming, fine-grained pottery. Chinese porcelains made hundreds of years ago are treasured all over the world.

Some very early Chinese artists used rows of small drawings of objects to record messages. As these drawings were repeated over and over, they were gradually changed into patterns of lines called characters. Each character represented a word in this kind of writing. Characters are still in use for writing in China today.

A standardized set of characters that one could memorize and learn to read and to write was developed under the Ch'in dynasty about 200 B.C. The Ch'in rulers are also remembered because they were the first to expand the kingdom into a broader empire. And it was they who started to build the Great Wall of China to protect their northern borders from invaders. The two Ch'in emperors ruled only a

The Great Wall of China, built by the Ch'in emperors thousands of years ago, still stands.

few years, but we know the whole country by their name today.

It was fine to have a way to write and read the Chinese language. But having to memorize a character for each of hundreds of words took a great deal of time and effort. In the families of the nobles and the rich landowners, there was plenty of time for young men to study. But the common people had to work hard and long to have enough to eat, a place to sleep, and something to wear. Very few of them had time or opportunity to memorize all those characters. So reading and writing were skills only a privileged few people could hope to master. To most of the Chinese, the characters seemed mysterious and wonderful. Scholars who understood them were very much respected.

Confucius and the Rule of Scholars

About 2,500 years ago a scholar named Kung Fu-tzu, "Kung the Master," became very well known as a teacher and as an official of the government. In the West he is known as Confucius.

Confucius taught that rulers must be good examples of right living if they wanted their country to prosper. He also taught that every man should be kind, upright, polite, and wise. He should honor his parents and ancestors, do his duty to the state, and be faithful.

That sounds like good advice for any people or time. But Confucius also believed that only men who had had time and opportunity to study could be leaders. He had little respect for the working people who kept the country going. He felt that the educated would naturally have the high positions and those who had not been educated would naturally be downtrodden. Since there were very few schools and a family had to have some wealth to be able to send a son to school, the poor had no hope of advancement.

Moreover, Confucius assumed that boys and men were the only people of any importance. He taught that girls should obey their fathers; as married women they should obey their husbands; and as old women they should obey their sons.

For many hundreds of years, these teachings of Confucius were the foundation of life in China. Posts in the government were granted on the basis of examinations that were open only to scholars. Men who won government posts became part of a group which had great power and often used it selfishly. Workers, farmers, and soldiers, who had no chance for schooling, were looked down upon. They were harshly treated, and often they and their families suffered and starved.

As for girls and women, they had a very low place in Chinese life. Sometimes newborn girls were simply drowned to get rid of them. If hard times struck, girl children were often sold by their fathers. Even in wealthy families women had almost no rights.

Workers, farmers, and soldiers are the most important groups in today's China. The teachings of Confucius have been discarded, and people young and old criticize him and modern leaders who seem to follow his ideas.

"Knowledge comes from practice, not just from books," is a saying of today. Everyone— girls as well as boys—goes to school. Everyone learns to read and write, with the letters of the Western alphabet as well as Chinese characters. But everyone also has practice working on a farm and in a factory. Farms, factories, schools, and neighborhoods are all run by committees on which both men and women serve. Women as well as men can become leaders.

"Women can prop up half the sky," the Chinese say today, with pride.

3. Land of Mountains and Rivers

For more than 3,000 years, China has existed as a great nation in East Asia. It is bordered on the east by the China Seas, whose waters flow into the Pacific Ocean. On the inland sides, circling mountains cut it off from its neighbors.

Today the People's Republic of China is the third largest nation on earth. It is smaller only than the Union of Soviet Socialist Republics and Canada. It is larger than the United States of America. And it has more people than those three other giants together. China has one-fourth of all the people on earth.

China has not always been so large and

populous. Since the early centuries when the kingdom first arose in the basin of the Hwang Ho, or Yellow River, its borders have stretched many times. Sometimes, under weak kings or emperors, the borders have shrunk.

Rulers have from time to time built new capital cities. But most of the time China's capital has been in the old heart of the country, in the valley of the Hwang Ho, as Peking is today.

Present-day China is not quite as large as it was about 200 years ago. But it stretches 3,000 miles from the high country of Tibet in the west to the farthest eastern point of Manchuria. And from the northern boundary of Manchuria to the southern tip of Hainan Island in the South China Sea is about 2,500 miles.

River Valleys

Much of China's best farmland lies in the valleys of three great river systems. In the northeast is the Hwang Ho. South of it the mighty Yangtze winds across the country from west to east for more than 3,200 miles. And among the tumble of hills and valleys in the south China countryside flow the streams that feed the Si-kiang, or West River, system.

Most of China's people live crowded into the

plains watered by these great rivers. But the rivers have been a mixed blessing to them.

The 2,700-mile-long Hwang Ho, or Yellow River, has been called "China's sorrow" because its floods have done so much damage to crops and homes. In recent years, "since Liberation" as the Communists like to say, dams and power plants have been built along the Hwang Ho. More are planned. New canals have been dug. The river channel has been walled with stone along dangerous stretches. So floods are no longer a serious problem, and the waters can be better used for irrigation.

Work is underway to tame the Yangtze River, too, and the Huai River, which flows into the Yangtze from the north. The Huai, which forms a boundary between the drier, colder north China and the moister, warmer south, has also been feared for its floods. But now it is being brought under control, along with the Yangtze.

The Yangtze rises among 20,000-foot peaks in Tibet. During its long journey across China, it waters one-quarter of all the country's farmland. One-third of China's people live within the basin of this mighty river system.

One of the most thickly populated sections

Wuchang, one of the Han cities, clings to the side of a mountain overlooking the Yangtze.

is in the high country around the city of Chungking. This inland port city is built high on the rocky river banks. It is the shipping point for crops of the fertile farming area around Chungking.

The river channel twists through narrow gorges walled with steep cliffs. Until recently night travel on the upper reaches of the Yangtze was forbidden by law. For the water spun and bubbled around dangerous rocks that poked up above the surface. Boats had to be dragged upstream through these gorges by lines of men tugging on ropes as they moved along towpaths on the shore. Sometimes the towpath was a narrow, slippery shelf of rock cut into the steep bank. These stretches were dangerous for the men on shore as well as for those on the boats.

Now rocks in treacherous shallows have been dynamited. Buoys bob on the surface of the river to mark the safe channel and to warn of reefs. Some curving stretches have been straightened with huge amounts of labor. So boats no longer have to tie up at the bank when darkness falls.

Hundreds of miles downstream, the river widens as other streams join it from the north and south. When mountain snows melt and water from spring rains floods the river beds, the largest lakes in China spread over the low-lying fields. At high water the largest of these, Tungting Hu, covers an area three-fourths the size of the state of Connecticut. In the winter much of the lake bed is dry enough to grow a good crop of rice.

This rich land has supported many people for more than 2,000 years. Busy cities have grown up at the river junction. Three of them together are called Wuhan, "the Han cities." Even years ago seagoing ships could travel almost 600 miles up the Yangtze to Wuhan.

There goods going farther inland had to be transferred to barges or small, mat-roofed sampans for the more difficult upstream stretch.

Downstream, as it flows toward the sea, the Yangtze reaches the lowlands. Here it spreads out and slows its pace as it travels through rich farming country. This delta land is dotted with cities and towns large and small. Two of the largest are Shanghai and Nanking. Between them are the farm villages of rural communes. Wherever one looks, small homes dot the fields. And this delta is growing. The Yangtze carries so much sand and soil on its journey to the sea that its droppings push the delta forward about 60 feet a year.

Travel and transport of goods in early China depended almost entirely on rivers rather than roads. But both the Hwang Ho and the Yangtze flow generally from west to east. There was no way to travel north or south by water. A waterway to connect the major rivers was badly needed. Almost 2,500 years ago an emperor started the construction of a great canal to link those two river basins. It was more than 1,700 years before this huge engineering project, called the Grand Canal, was completed. When it was finished, it was 1,000 miles long.

Trains of sampans and gilded royal barges moved slowly up and down this gently curving inland waterway for hundreds of years. All the principal towns along the canal had inns where travelers could stop.

In modern times the railways have taken over much of the transport of goods. Some sections of the canal have become clogged with silt. But on other stretches there is a good deal of slow-moving boat traffic even today.

Hills and Mountains

The Grand Canal runs through rich farmland. But there is not very much of that in China. Eighty-five percent of the country is covered with mountains too rough for farming or is too high or too dry to raise good crops.

The mountains start close to the coast in the south. Here the country is so rough that many small groups of people have lived in small pockets of land, cut off from their neighbors, for hundreds of years.

Toward the west the whole country rises. And the mountains rise to join towering ranges. Many of the loftiest peaks in the world are found in the Himalayas, which separate China from India to the south. In the north the Tien

In the valleys of Tibet, wheat for China's people is now harvested with the help of giant combines.

Shan range towers between China and the Soviet Union.

On China's side of the rugged mountain border lie the areas known as the autonomous (self-governing) regions of Tibet and Sinkiang. Much of Tibet is 15,000 or 16,000 feet above sea level. It is covered with chains of snow-peaked mountains with high valleys between. Rivers have cut some of the valleys into impassable gorges, so travel is very difficult.

North of Tibet lies vast, almost empty Sinkiang. It too has great mountains which divide it almost in two, with deserts to the north and south. These deserts have never been able to provide a living to many people.

East of Sinkiang lies Inner Mongolia, where some of the driest land in the world is to be found. This is the Gobi Desert, a place of sandy plains and wind-heaped dunes.

These high desolate lands were first claimed by China more than 2,000 years ago. But they never were of much interest to most Chinese. Only under the Communists has an effort been made to plant trees for lumber and fruit and to expand farming. Groups of young Chinese are sent to work in these lands, among people who speak different languages and have their own time-honored ways of living.

It is hard for some of the young people from China to settle down so far from their old homes and friends. It is also hard for the people of these border lands to accept new ways of doing things and to give up the religion and customs which have meant so much to them. But new roads and airlines form links. They help to bind together widely separated peoples and kinds of countryside into one great land of mountains and rivers, the People's Republic of China.

4. The Middle Kingdom and the World Beyond

Through most of their long history, the people of China and their rulers have cared little about the world outside. They loved China's craggy mountains, its rich plains, and its rivers rushing toward some distant sea. They felt that their land was the center of the world and that anything beyond its borders must be inferior. The "Middle Kingdom," as they called their country, was enough for them.

Trade by Land and Sea

A few foreigners were permitted to enter China if they brought rich gifts and bowed down to the Chinese rulers. Most of these foreigners were traders, and some of the goods they brought did please the proud Chinese.

From about 200 B.C. until about 200 years after the time of Christ, the Han dynasty ruled China. Its emperors enjoyed foreign goods. They also liked to use their royal power. So they sent conquering armies far to the northwest, across the lands now called Mongolia and Sinkiang. Thanks to their conquests, they established a safe route for trading caravans to travel across Central Asia.

For centuries lines of laden camels and donkeys carried silks and porcelains from China across the long overland trails to Persia and the "sunset lands" beyond. On their return journeys the caravans brought spices and glassware from the eastern Mediterranean, grapevines from Persia, and swift and powerful horses from Mongolia.

Some traders also reached China by sea. Roman galleys and, later, square-beamed Arabic dhows sailed the long sea route to southern Chinese ports. Sometimes on their return journeys, the ships carried officials of the Chinese court on visits to Western rulers. These pleasant contacts began during the 300-year rule of the T'ang emperors, from about 600 to 900, and continued during the rule of the Sung emperors.

But while China was prospering, developing in peaceful arts and sciences and education, a new warlike power was rising in the harsh lands to the north, beyond the Great Wall. This power was the Mongol army of horsemen under their fierce and bold leader, Genghis Khan.

Sweeping down from their grasslands, the Mongols broke through the earth-and-stone barrier of the Great Wall to conquer Peking in the north of China. Part of their army stayed, and some years later under Kublai Khan, a grandson of Genghis Khan, they overcame southern China too.

The Mongol dynasty, known as the Yuan, ruled China for about a hundred years. At the same time other Mongol armies were riding westward from their Mongolian homeland. They conquered Russia and the Middle East and threatened Europe.

These Mongol rulers did not care about the sea. But they prided themselves on keeping the overland trade routes open and safe across all their vast domain. It was along one of these routes that the Italian trader Marco Polo trav-

Near Peking, where Mongol emperors once ruled, caravans are still used to transport goods.

eled to the splendid court of Kublai Khan. And his tales of life there made the kingdom of Cathay, as he called China, famous in Europe.

By the time the Mongol dynasty was overthrown in China, their power to control the routes across Central Asia was weakening too. Soon the overland routes became dangerous. Caravans could no longer be sure of safe passage. Trade declined, and it was missed by the wealthy Chinese who had liked to amuse themselves with purchases from distant lands.

To replace the overland routes, emperors of the Ming dynasty—which had overthrown the Mongols—sent out fleets of ships. They crossed southern waters as far away as Java, Malaya, Ceylon, and India. Rounding the tip of India, some ships pushed on to Red Sea ports and cities on the east coast of Africa.

From one of these voyages to Africa, the sailors even brought back a giraffe as a gift to the emperor.

For some years the sea trade was brisk. Then a new Ming emperor came to the throne. His officials were jealous of the commanders of the fleet. Also, like many Chinese, they did not really like the sea. So they persuaded the new emperor to disband the fleet and put a stop to the trade. China once again retreated within its own boundaries.

Europe Reaches Out

By this time—the mid-1400s—rulers and nobles in Europe had come to like Chinese tea, silks, and porcelains. They also liked spices for their food. Many of these spices came from islands called the Indies in the South China Sea. So ships and sailors set out from the seaports of Europe in search of routes to the Spice

Islands and the mysterious land they knew as Cathay.

Before the 1400s were over, bold Portuguese sailors had circled Africa and reached India. Christopher Columbus, sailing under the flag of Spain, had found in the western ocean some islands he thought were the Indies. They came to be called the West Indies. And by 1514 a Portuguese merchant sailing on a Chinese ship reached the south China port of Kwangchow, or Canton.

Dutch, French, and British traders followed during the next century. But the men who advised the Chinese emperor were suspicious of foreigners and did not welcome them. Though the trade brought rich stores of silver to China, foreign ships were permitted to dock only in the harbor they called Canton. And crew men and merchants could not move freely even there. They could not even spend a night in the city.

Years passed. The Ming emperors grew weak, and invaders from Manchuria in the north took over the rule of China. These Manchu rulers, who came to be known as the Ch'ing dynasty, shared the old Chinese mistrust of foreigners. They did not even trust many Chinese. So they kept Western traders under tight control during stops in China. And they did not permit Chinese people to travel abroad.

The Manchu rulers were successful in adding to their territory. By about 1800 they had pushed out in many directions so that more land was under the control of China than ever before. But of what was going on in the rest of the world they knew and cared little.

By this time in Europe and North America, machines powered by steam engines were changing the methods of producing goods. The use of machines was beginning to change methods of growing and harvesting crops. And the spread of democracy began to change the relationship between governments and their people. China, however, having closed its doors to the Western world, was cut off from these changes.

Life in China went on much as it had for thousands of years. During the long, peaceful reigns of some early Manchu emperors, new industries were started, and farm crops improved. But unfortunately people raised larger families, and the population grew much faster than food production. So by the early 1800s there was more suffering in China than ever before.

The Curse of Opium

The rulers, nobles, landlords, and the other wealthy families of China lived in large homes, beautifully furnished. Servants cooked splendid meals for them. The rich wore robes of heavy silk, often richly embroidered. And as a sign that they never needed to work with their hands, they let their fingernails grow very long.

At the same time millions of other Chinese had only rags to wear and very little food to eat. They slept on thin mats on cold mud floors. If they had jobs, they were forced to work long, hard hours, with no thought given to their safety or welfare. If they had no work, they and their families were likely to starve.

There was little comfort or joy in life for most of the Chinese people. One way they could escape from their troubles was by buying small tablets of opium to smoke in small pipes.

Opium has been used as a medicine for many hundreds of years. The sticky brownish gum is the dried juice of a certain kind of poppy. Doctors in China, as in other lands, knew it was valuable for the relief of pain and to bring on sleep. But they also knew that it was very dangerous.

Opium is very habit-forming. It can ruin one's health and cause death.

One of the places where the opium poppy used to grow well was India. By 1750 the British controlled much of India. When they found that opium was widely used by doctors in China, they sensed a profitable new trade. They had many acres planted in these poppies. Soon they were shipping the gum to China by the chestful—hundreds of large chests a year.

With so much opium available, dealers did not wait for doctors to send patients to buy a little as medicine. They began to sell it to anyone who wanted to get away from his troubles for a few hours and have a pleasant dream.

As more and more Chinese got the opium habit, the market grew. By the early 1800s, thousands of chests a year were shipped to China. Now the British traders could buy all the silks and tea and porcelains and lacquered screens they wanted. The money they received for opium more than paid for all these luxuries. In addition silver began to flow out of China to enrich British traders.

The Manchu emperor and his officials were disturbed by this loss of wealth. They were also concerned about the effect opium was having on the health of millions of Chinese people. An official of the court wrote to Queen Victoria of England and demanded that the wicked and vicious people who "beguile the Chinese people into a death trap" be stopped. He asked that the opium traffic be cut off and that the valleys of India be sown in wholesome grain instead.

The traffic was not stopped. The emperor ordered an official to seize a large stock of the forbidden drug. The British protested and sailed into Chinese ports with gunboats. The Chinese, who had almost no navy, were quickly defeated.

Canton in 1800. Foreign trading stations lined the shore; foreign ships anchored in the harbor.

As a result of this defeat, the Chinese were forced to pay Britain a huge sum in silver. They also had to sign a treaty in 1842, the first of many such, opening their country to trade.

The ports where this trade was carried on became known as Treaty Ports. In them Chinese law had no power over foreigners. The foreign businessmen lived in special areas of the cities known as "foreign concessions." They had to pay only a very small tax on goods they sold in China.

Several times during the 20 years after the Opium War, Britain and France used gunboats to force China to open additional ports to trade and to pay more silver. Eventually there were more than 90 of these treaty ports in China, far up inland rivers as well as on the coasts.

The series of "unequal treaties" marked the start of a century of lively Western trade with China. The trade brought wealth to Chinese merchants as well as to the traders of Britain, France, the United States, and other countries. To the mass of people in China, however, it brought only troubles: higher taxes, loss of national dignity, and a weakening of government.

5. The People Rise

Taxes in China went up, up, up. Tax collectors demanded of the farmers much more than they were supposed to collect for the government. The additional money they kept for themselves. More and more poor farmers lost their land because they could not pay these unfair sums.

Many of these poor families drifted to cities to try to find a new way to live. There they saw the ruling class of Chinese and the haughty foreigners living very well indeed. In their minds, the poor people linked the foreigners with the wealthy Chinese as being the cause of their woes. And bitterness against both groups grew in their hearts.

It was not only farm families who were having bitter times. Another group were the porters who had formerly carried the silks, tea, and other trade goods south to Canton over inland roads. As new treaty ports were opened farther north, goods no longer had to be carried long distances to the south. This meant that porters and dock workers in Canton were left with no way to make a living.

At this time a leader arose in south China who claimed to have been sent by heaven to drive out the wicked rulers. Many of the desperate poor of China flocked to follow him. He and his supporters set out to conquer the country. They set up the "Heavenly Kingdom of Equality," *Tai ping tian guo* in Chinese, with a capital in the city of Nanking.

This Tai ping government, as it was known, introduced reforms based on Christian principles, including granting rights to women. It lasted for eleven years, from 1853 to 1864. Then the Europeans joined forces with the Manchus to overthrow the Tai ping.

The Heavenly Kingdom is remembered in China today as the first of many uprisings. It showed that the common people were beginning to feel their strength. And it did cause the Manchu emperors to start modernizing their rule in some ways.

One thing that made many modern advances difficult in China was the old belief in the power of spirits. People honored—and feared—the spirits of the land, the mountains, and the rivers, and of their ancestors. People were afraid that building railways might disturb the graves of ancestors. The building of bridges might anger river spirits. Digging mines for mineral wealth might anger the spirits of the earth and mountains, it was thought.

Despite these fears, some bridges and railways were built. Some mines were opened. And the rulers decided to build a modern navy, since they blamed earlier defeats on lack of sea power.

A modern navy needed more than new ships. Officers had to be trained in handling the ships. Young men had to be sent abroad for this training. For the first time in many years, groups of bright young Chinese men had glimpses of the outside world. Soon other young men whose families had money were also going abroad to study. They came back with bold ideas for change in their homeland.

Empress Dowager Tzu-hsi ruled China for almost a half century.

Meanwhile the Manchu rulers lost more and more of their power and territory. In the south, China had had influence over the territory now know as Laos, Cambodia, and Vietnam. France seized this area. Japan pushed China out of Taiwan and Korea. Russia began to edge in from the northeast. And by 1900 the countries of Europe were drawing their own maps of the Middle Kingdom itself, with the entire country divided among them into "spheres of influence."

In Peking a powerful woman of the Manchu court, Empress Dowager Tzu-hsi, put her nephew on the throne as emperor. But she was the

54

power behind the throne. She stamped out attempts by the young emperor and his friends to modernize the country. Instead she befriended another secret society, "The Fist of Righteous Harmony," more widely known as the Boxers. This group was filled with deep hatred of all foreigners. The dowager empress opened the gates of the Imperial City of Peking to them, and they surrounded all the foreign legations— the headquarters of European nations in the capital. The Boxers fought desperately to drive all the hated "barbarians" from the country.

The foreigners, threatened with losing their hold on China, joined together to take Peking. And they forced upon the weak Manchu rulers another harsh treaty. A few years later both the empress dowager and the young captive emperor died, and the rule of the Manchus approached its end.

A Rocky Road to Freedom

In the early 1900s young men arriving home in China from schools in Europe or the United States looked around them unhappily. Near the docks they saw hollow-cheeked beggars; some holding sickly babies. In the shadows of business buildings, they saw homeless people lying

55

on the pavement, dying or dead. Soon they encountered bribe-taking officials and cheating tax collectors.

Many of these educated young men decided that something had to be done to change Chinese society and to give the common people a chance. Revolutionary groups, led by students returning from foreign universities, sprang up in many cities. The head of this movement was a young doctor, Sun Yat-sen by name. For many years he had to work from outside China, to avoid imprisonment. But within China the movement grew. Many workers joined. And many young army officers also felt that the weak old dynasty must go.

It was a revolt by the army officers that finally drove out the Manchus. And a general named Yuan was elected the first president of the new Republic of China in 1912, when Dr. Sun stepped aside in his favor.

It soon became clear that what this general wanted was to become emperor himself. That was the way many dynasties had come to power in the past. The army officers did not realize that there was a new spirit in China.

General Yuan did not succeed in his plan to set up a new dynasty. But he did keep the new republic from getting a firm start. Yuan soon died, but for ten years after that, various warlords continued to struggle for power.

No one really won a lasting victory. But the losers in the struggle were the Chinese people, as bands of soldiers roamed the countryside— burning, looting, and stealing crops.

During this disorderly time two groups grew stronger. One was the Nationalist Party, called the Kuomintang, led by Dr. Sun Yat-sen. Dr. Sun and his friends still had high hopes for a democratic Republic of China. For several brief periods Dr. Sun was president of the republic. But in order to gain and hold any power among the battling warlords, he had to have army support too. When he died in 1925 it was one of these soldiers, Chiang Kai-shek, who became the leader of the Kuomintang.

The other group that was gaining strength during these troubled years in China was the Communist Party. The Communist Party in China was organized in 1921 by a small group of young men. One of them was named Mao Tse-tung.

At the same time a group of young Chinese studying in Paris formed a Communist Party unit. One of these young men was Chou

En-lai. They were to become two of the most powerful men in the new China. But before that happened they had some very hard times.

One big problem was friction with the Kuomintang. Communists believe that all land and houses, all farms and factories, stores, railways, and other means of transportation and production should belong to the state—to all the people—rather than to a few individuals. They believe that everyone should work for the state, wherever he or she is needed, doing whatever needs to be done for the good of all.

The Kuomintang knew that changes were needed, but they did not want to overturn all the ways of living. And by 1927 it was the Kuomintang which controlled most of China. The capital of the republic was in Nanking, but the country was really run by wealthy businessmen in Shanghai. The poor people were no better off than they had been under the emperors.

For a few years the Communists in China cooperated with the Kuomintang. Both groups accepted aid and advice from the Communist Soviet Union. But the Communists felt that Chiang Kai-shek and his Kuomintang party had betrayed the people and the spirit of the revolution. The two groups split apart with great bitterness.

Chiang Kai-shek had his armies kill as many of the Communists as they could find. Those who escaped had a difficult time. They fled to the southern mountains. From a base there they reached out into the countryside, got rid of landlords, and divided the large estates among the peasants. Countless peasants became grateful supporters of the Communists.

Chinese Communist troops in Yenan training for action during the late 1930s

Gradually the Communists took over a whole southern province, Kiangsi, which they called the Chinese Soviet Republic. Chiang Kai-shek could not stand for that. He had his troops blockade the roads into the province so that no salt or other supplies could reach it. No people can live for very long without salt. So the Communist soldiers and their followers had to break through the Kuomintang's blockade in order to survive.

For a year they marched across country. They waded through marshes. They tramped across high, windy plains where there were no roads or villages. They climbed snowy mountain slopes. Tens of thousands died along the way. But in October 1934 about 20,000 Communists reached safety in a poor mountain region far to the north, among friendly peasants of Yenan in Shensi province.

The Long March—6,000 miles—was over. But it has lived on in song and story. Those who marched are heroes of today's China.

More Warfare

In the 1930s the Japanese pushed their way through Manchuria in the north and deep into the heart of China. Chiang Kai-shek and his

Kuomintang government did little to fight the Japanese. Instead they retreated far to the west. In the area around Chungking, where they set up their new capital, taxes were cruelly high and peasants were terribly poor. The Kuomintang seemed to be accepting this harsh old kind of government.

Meanwhile in the north the Communists, with many new recruits from the peasants they had helped, fought the invaders wherever and whenever they could. This won more people to their side. By 1945, when World War II ended, the Communists controlled half of China.

Civil warfare continued to rage between the Communists and the Kuomintang. The Kuomintang had better equipment, including airplanes. But the Communists had the spirit of the people behind them. The Communist armies moved southward, and by mid-1949 they had won south China too. Chiang Kai-shek and his remaining forces fled to the island of Taiwan with whatever treasure they could carry. There they set up a Kuomintang, or Nationalist, government. Back in Peking, on October 1, 1949, Mao Tse-tung proclaimed from the gate of the Imperial Palace the birth of the People's Republic of China.

6. Dictatorship of the Common Man

Fireworks glowed and flashed in the dark skies over many Chinese cities one evening in January 1975. The Chinese radio broadcast lively patriotic songs, and newscasters had good news to announce. The National People's Congress had just met in the Great Hall of the People in Peking. And it had adopted a newly revised constitution for the nation.

Next day red posters were pasted up on walls all over China. In big bold characters they spread the word of the new constitution to those who had not been listening to the radio news.

The constitution had been worked out by the Central Committee of the Communist Party, the only important political party of China today.

"The Communist Party of China is the core of leadership of the whole Chinese people," says the new constitution. And after 25 years the Chairman of the party was still Mao Tse-tung, who had announced the birth of the People's Republic. Although he was too elderly to be very active anymore, Mao Tse-tung was still looked up to, and his teachings were quoted all over China.

When small children learn to write in school, one of the first sentences they learn to form is, "We love Chairman Mao." And a favorite song and dance of kindergarten youngsters tells about the joy of going to visit Chairman Mao.

The Road to Leadership

Chairman Mao rose to power through the Communist Party. And even today the best way to become a leader in the People's Republic of China is to be active in the Party.

As a start, most children join the Little Red Soldiers in primary school. Classmates discuss whether each boy and girl has the right attitudes at work and play to make a good Little

Red Soldier. These attitudes include a spirit of helpfulness and cooperation. But most important is working for the state.

In their teens the most active Little Red Soldiers become Red Guards. And as adults they may finally join the Communist Party.

The next step toward leadership is membership on a revolutionary committee. Every factory, rural commune, neighborhood, school, and town has one of these committees to supervise it. A factory committee has workers on it. A rural commune committee has farmers. And a school committee includes both teachers and students.

Ideally every committee should have young, middle-aged, and older members. But every committee also includes members known as "cadres." They have been appointed because they are good Party members. They make sure that people do not work for personal profit or power instead of for the good of the state.

From the local revolutionary committees some people advance to the committees in charge of whole provinces. The next step is membership in the national Communist Party Congress. There are about 1,000 members of this Congress. About 300 of them are chosen to sit on the Central Committee of the Communist Party. This was the group that worked out the new constitution. The leaders of the Central Committee form the Political Bureau, which runs the powerful Communist Party. And at the top is the Chairman, one of the most powerful men in the country.

People's Congresses

The actual government of the People's Republic is organized very much like the Communist Party. Every town and rural commune has a People's Congress. Almost everyone who is at least eighteen years of age can vote for members of the local congress. But the voters do not have much choice, since the names on the ballot are chosen in discussions among the local members of the Communist Party.

Deputies—members—of the local People's Congress choose representatives to the Provincial Congress. There are 21 provinces. Peking and Shanghai rank as independent cities. And there are also five autonomous regions whose people are mainly non-Chinese. They have Congresses too. Each Provincial Congress chooses representatives to the National People's Congress.

The more than 3,000 deputies in the National People's Congress are elected for five-year terms. They represent every area of the country. National minority groups—tribes and other peoples who are not traditionally Chinese—are well represented. And a few people are given seats just because they are outstanding patriots.

The local and provincial congresses meet a few days each year. They appoint People's Committees to carry on the work of government the rest of the time.

The National Congress is a largely honorary body. It may hold a session each year, but it does not always do so. Since it does not have real duties, several years may pass between sessions. This happened during the years when the revised constitution was being considered.

The constitution was sent to the Congresses in all the provinces and regions. These groups had time to discuss it before their delegates to the National People's Congress were called to Peking to vote approval.

Between sessions of the National Congress the day-to-day work of the national government is carried on under the leadership of the Standing Committee of the Congress and the State Council.

At home, at work, and in public places, the ideas of
Chairman Mao dominate the lives of the Chinese.

The Standing Committee of the National People's Congress handles relations with other countries and interprets laws at home. It also decides when the full Congress shall meet.

The State Council is something like the president's cabinet in the United States or the prime minister's in England or Canada. The ministers who make up the Council are in charge of the various departments of the government. The premier, or prime minister, and several vice premiers also are in the State Council. They are all people who have been well recommended by the Central Committee of the Communist Party.

Government by Discussion

The new constitution says, "The People's Republic of China is a dictatorship of the people, based on the alliance of workers and peasants." Decisions come from above, it is explained, but ideas come from below—from the common people. It is through discussions, debates, and public criticism that these ideas come out and people have their say.

The constitution states that the people must have the right to speak out freely, to air their views fully, to hold great debates, and even to write "big character posters" criticizing leaders who, they feel, have done wrong.

But people realize that they must be careful about their criticism of leaders. In 1957 Chairman Mao invited criticism, and many people responded. The springing up of new ideas was called "The Spring of a Hundred Flowers." But it did not last.

Those who seemed to be criticizing the principles of Communism soon found themselves working in mines or in dreary areas far from their homes. Most of the criticisms came from members of the educated group, rather than the workers and peasants who are the backbone of Communism. Today there is little criticism of the government.

Criticisms and discussions are used a great deal, though, among people who study or work or live together.

In school one or two youngsters may not get along well with the group. Then a discussion is held, often in the classroom. Other students tell the wrongdoer what they think of his problem. They encourage him to criticize himself. Then he, or she, usually understands and determines to mend his, or her, ways.

In a factory there may be a dispute between

a worker and his foreman. Members of the revolutionary committee in charge of the factory organize a discussion group. Coworkers listen to both sides of the argument. They help the people who differ to agree on the best way to proceed.

In a family there may be a sharp difference of opinion between the mother and father. The revolutionary committee of the neighborhood arranges for neighbors to talk the problem over with the pair. Usually it can be settled amiably.

There may be someone who does not truly believe in Communism and who does not work for the success of the government and the good of the state. Such a person may be deprived of political rights for a time. He will be given opportunities to discuss his problem with others. After a period of retraining in proper thinking and some time spent working in a factory or on a rural commune, usually such a person is brought into line. For working with one's hands for the state is the foundation of Chinese life today.

7. Agriculture, Foundation of the State

Down a country road in China, men trudge slowly, pushing hand carts loaded high. Here the loads are bamboo stalks, but many kinds of goods are moved along the roads by man or woman power. Along a shallow canal a flat barge drifts as a boy lifts his pushing pole from the muddy bottom. On the bank of the canal, women jog in single file, each with a pair of baskets swinging from the ends of her shoulder yoke.

There are some machines on China's farms, but not many. Most of the work is done by the strong arms and legs and backs of the people.

China has more than 800 million people, and four out of every five of them live in the countryside. They spend most of their working hours raising food.

Feeding 800 million people is a tremendous task. Through much of China's history, feeding all her people has proved impossible. When the rains failed or floods washed out the fields and destroyed crops, there were often famines.

In the old China of the emperors, most of the land (80 percent) was owned by a few (7 percent) of the people. Most of the farm workers owned no land. They worked on the large estates for the barest of livings. Often they did not have enough to eat. Their dream was of owning their own plots of land and of being able to work for themselves.

Farms to Communes

As the Communists rose to power, they began to seize estates from landowners. They distributed the land among the farm workers. This seemed a dream come true for many of the country folk, and they flocked to the support of the Communists.

Having each farmer own and work his own small plot is not really the Communist way, though. Communists believe that all the means of production should belong to all the people together—to the state.

When the People's Republic came into being in 1949, the leaders of the Communist Party soon went to work toward their goal of state ownership. First they asked the farmers to share their tasks by joining teams to help one another. These mutual aid teams made farm work a bit more efficient.

Next the Communists asked the farmers to join cooperatives. Most of the country men could see an advantage to this—marketing crops together and buying seed and other supplies in large quantities at lower prices.

A few years later the farmers were told to give their land to much larger cooperatives. These were called communes. All the land was to be jointly held. All the farmers would work for the commune and be paid for their work.

This was a difficult step for many of the country people who had dreamed so long of owning their own land. But they did turn over their land to the state. The step-by-step change from small private farms to communes was completed in 1958.

The members of a commune were to share

more than their land and their work, though, the government said. They were also to give up living as families. All cooking tools were to be turned over to communal dining halls, and all meals were to be eaten there. Children were to be cared for by the commune. Men could be sent to work on other communes far from their families.

The rural people of China have always had strong family ties. This was too much for them to accept. They were so unhappy over this plan that their work was affected. In addition, floods and dry spells caused poor crops for several years. At last the government relented in part. Today family groups live in their own small homes on most rural communes. And the communes are smaller and more personal than was originally planned.

Organizing a Commune

There are more than 74,000 communes in China. They differ in many ways from one another. The crops they grow depend upon their location. Handicrafts are related to the old customs of the people. Most communes have some factories and workshops as well as fields, hothouses, and pens for chickens and pigs.

A production team works at assembling small machinery in this commune factory.

What is made in the factories is planned to fill the needs of the region. But all communes are similar in their organization.

Every commune is run by a revolutionary committee. Men and women work together on these committees. Under their leadership each commune is organized into brigades. Usually there are about 20 brigades on a commune. Each brigade is made up of about ten teams. Twelve or fifteen households make up a team.

Each worker is given work points for his hours of labor. Women work in the fields and workshops with the men. They get work points for this. The women also prepare meals and do other housework, but they do not receive work points for housework.

Most households have small private plots of land, often in the form of long, narrow strips. People, working in their spare time, grow vegetables on this land for their own use. If their crops are good, they may have some extra vegetables to sell in a nearby town.

Some people work in factories instead of fields. One rural commune, for example, has a workshop in which electric motors are assembled. It also has a carpet factory in which beautiful Chinese carpets are loomed by hand. In a nearby building, young women work at sewing machines making clothing and decorating cloth with colorful embroideries.

During the winters, especially in north China, there is less farm work to be done. Then many of the people on the communes work at handicrafts. Women knit sweaters and long, bright scarves. Men saw and hammer and carve, making toys and other small objects of wood.

On some communes the craftsmen can sell their craft work and keep the money for themselves. On other communes this income goes to the workers' brigade.

Most of the farm produce and the products made in the commune workshops are sold to the government. The revolutionary committee handles all the business arrangements. The committee pays the expenses of running the farm and workshops, the schools and clinics. They pay the taxes, which are low because the government is eager to bring rural incomes up toward city standards.

The money that is left after all expenses have been paid is divided as salaries. Salaries are paid on the basis of the work points each person has earned. The average income of a farm worker is about 300 yuan a year, whereas the average income of a factory worker in town is about 660 yuan a year. Selling vegetables and fruits from private plots, and an occasional pig fattened with kitchen scraps, may add about ten percent to a farm family's income. Of course there is usually more than one worker in a family, in the country or city.

Fields and Crops

Food crops—rice, grain, and vegetables—are grown on 90 percent of China's farm acres. Tea bushes cover many of the slopes in the southern half of the country. And fruits of all kinds, from grapes and apples to bananas and watermelons, are grown too.

The most popular meats are pork and duck. So most families keep a pig or two, and many communes raise them in large numbers. Ducks can be seen swimming in every pond and in many streams and canals. Most rural communes have a pond in which they raise fish and shrimp for food. They also breed chickens. And large numbers of cattle and sheep graze on the high, dry western grasslands.

Ten percent of China's farm acres are planted in cotton, jute, and hemp for coarse cloth and rope, and in trees for use in industry.

Quotations from Mao Tse-tung inspire the farm workers on this commune to work harder.

With more and more people, China must grow more and more food to feed them and cotton to clothe them. More acres of farmland are needed, but the land that can easily be farmed has been cultivated for thousands of years. Most of the rest is too steep and rocky.

In the cold, dry northwest there are vast stretches of "empty land." Some people call these lands of Tibet and Sinkiang "the wild west" of China. Most of the families on these high grasslands had wandered with their flocks for uncounted years. It was hard to persuade many of them to join communes, to settle in villages, to grow unfamiliar crops, or to work in new factories.

A new spirit was needed in these frontier provinces. To provide it, young people from distant towns and communes were sent to these areas to work and to spread "the message of Tachai."

"Learn from Tachai"

"In agriculture, learn from Tachai," people say, quoting Chairman Mao.

Tachai was a small, poor hill village. It had only small scattered patches of land in the gullies on which food could be raised. Each peasant farmed his own tiny plot. Little rain fell on these plots. Crops more often than not withered and dried up before they ripened. When rain did fall, it often washed the thin soil away.

In 1953 the farmers of Tachai were asked to put their holdings together into a collective. Many of them had dreamed all their lives of owning their own property. It was not easy to persuade them to give it up. But they did.

Then the farmers discussed what was needed to improve their crops. The main needs, they decided, were bigger fields, level and rich, and a better supply of water. To achieve these goals meant "making the mountains bow their heads and the rivers give way." This seemed an impossible dream. But the Tachai brigades made that dream come true.

To tame the rivers meant building dams. The country folk hacked stones out of the rocky hills and carried them in shoulder-yoke baskets to the places upstream they had chosen for dams.

To make the mountains bow their heads meant slashing the tops of six hills. To do this the peasants dug lime and made their own explosives. These explosions tore loose whole

Farmers in a Yenan commune, men and women alike, work together to dig the foundations for houses.

hilltops. The loosened rock and soil was used to fill in gullies to form level fields. On other hillsides people piled up stones by hand to form sturdy walls. Then they filled in soil behind the walls to form level terraced plots.

At the start of their work the people of Tachai had almost no machines. They relied on their own strong arms and legs and backs—and hearts. Thanks to the water stored behind their dams and the good soil on their level fields, they soon had a few good crops. With part of the money from the crops, they bought some machines for the commune.

Not everything went smoothly. Ten years

after they had started work, great floods struck Tachai. Even the new dams could not stand before those rushing waters. Soil was washed away from the new fields. Houses collapsed.

The damage was a great blow to the people of Tachai. Some said, "Let us ask the government for money for rebuilding." Others said, "Let us go to work at other trades until we can get money to repair the dams and fields and houses." But people who believed in the Communist way of life were convinced that they could accomplish anything that was needed by working together. So they set to work to repair the damage. And they succeeded.

The story of Tachai is told wherever peasants feel regret at giving up their private farms to work together on a commune. It is told where people are spending too much work time on their private garden plots. "In agriculture, learn from Tachai" is a slogan known all over China.

Not everyone in the Chinese countryside has been won over completely to the Communist way of life. It is harder to change people's ways of thinking than to teach them to use new machines. But as crops improve and incomes rise through hard work on the communes, the "message of Tachai" is spreading.

8. Working in Industry for the Good of the State

Before the Communist era China had little industry. Most of the few factories that did exist produced silks and other goods to be sold outside the country. Machines and all sorts of heavy equipment had to be imported from other lands.

The profits earned by industry went to a few men, the factory owners. They became wealthy. As for the workers, they toiled long hours for very little pay. Many of them were children who had no one to care for them. No thought was given to their safety or health. They were not properly fed, and their clothes were rags.

Many of the child workers did not live to grow up. Those who are still alive today remember as symbols of their bitter past the bell and the clock. They remember the factory bell because it woke them before daylight from the sleep they needed. The clock is a hated memory because foremen often set the clock hands back during the work day to lengthen the hours of labor. It is not surprising that often the work was not efficiently done.

The Communists felt that the system was bad. When they came to power, they determined to change it. "The country must be self-reliant," the Party leaders announced. They set up the first of a series of Five Year Plans to bring this about.

The first Plan ran from 1953 through 1957. During these years all the factories were taken over from their owners. The former owners were offered a chance to stay on as employees, since experienced managers were needed. Some of them did stay on, at higher pay than ordinary workers received.

The government also established some new industries. The new leaders were eager to have China produce its own machine tools, mining equipment, trucks, and airplanes.

With the start of the Second Five Year Plan in 1958 the government announced that the country was to make a "Great Leap Forward." This was the signal for sweeping changes. One change was pulling all private farms into communes. Another was to introduce a great many people to industry.

People all over the country were urged to set up enterprises such as small blast furnaces. These backyard furnaces were to smelt iron ore and charcoal into pig iron. Many towns had small coal pits nearby that supplied fuel to fire

More than 20,000 people work in this large tractor factory in Honan Province.

the furnaces. But backyard smelters manned by inexperienced men did not prove to be successful, and they had to be given up.

Sweeping changes like this were too hastily tried in many fields. The Great Leap Forward really upset industry in China more than it helped. But it did introduce many people to basic methods of industrial production.

During this same period some huge factories were built with the help of experts from the Soviet Union. In 1960, however, a quarrel developed between China and the Soviet Union. All the Russian experts left the country. They left some projects half-finished and took the plans with them.

The Chinese managed to complete those projects. Since then they have favored the building of smaller factories, scattered widely through the countryside.

The Cultural Revolution

The Second Five Year Plan met its goals for farming and industry two years ahead of schedule. One group in the Chinese government thought this was splendid. They felt that the most important thing was to develop agriculture and industry as quickly as possible.

They favored letting educated young people push ahead as rapidly as they could, so their knowledge could be used to improve both crops and factory production.

Chairman Mao Tse-tung and his followers saw a danger in this. They too wanted production to increase on all fronts. But they did not want one group of educated people to gain too much power. They felt that the most important goal for China was rule by the common man.

Many young people agreed with this thinking. They felt that the schools and universities were being run to produce a small group of highly educated people. Those men and women would surge ahead to become leaders. They would soon consider themselves to be better than the workers and peasants. Then the country would be split again between the haves and the have-nots, as it had been under the emperors.

Young people in the teen-age organization called the Red Guards had angry discussions about this danger. They were encouraged by Chairman Mao. Soon they rose up as a disorderly young army. In 1966 they stormed onto railway trains and rode around the country spreading their ideas. This uprising was called the Great Proletarian Cultural Revolution.

A delegation of Red Guards on the move

On walls in cities and towns, they pasted posters criticizing leaders with whom they did not agree. They wrecked the offices of many government officials who differed with Mao Tse-tung. They rampaged through the universities and caused them to be closed for several years. In some provinces they so completely destroyed the local government that the army had to take over.

The Cultural Revolution succeeded in changing the school system. Today, students have a voice in all the planning of education. Workers and farmers and soldiers come into the schools to help the teachers. Students go out to factories and farms to work with and to learn from the workers and peasants.

To emphasize the placing of work above scholarship, school children and groups of workers have met to "criticize Lin Piao, Liu Shao, and Confucius." Even in kindergarten, children learn to recognize these three names. Lin Piao was one of the leaders who, some thought, wanted too much power for himself. Liu Shao favored letting educated young people push ahead and acquire positions of power. It was of course Confucius who long ago taught that the only route to the highest posts is through study.

In today's China, every kind of work has dignity. Everyone is supposed to work to serve the state, not to advance his or her own career. And the learning gained by working at a job is more highly valued than knowledge from books.

Industry Today

Chinese workers have responded to their new opportunities by increasing production. Many of the workers have developed improved methods or machines for their factories. And many of them help manage their factories.

All factories, like the farms, schools, and neighborhoods, are run by revolutionary committees. And workers are supposed to be able to criticize the management or members of the revolutionary committee. They also help decide on rewards for special contributions.

During the ten years from 1966 to 1975, industrial production in all fields more than doubled. China now exports more goods than it imports. Profits from these exports provide funds for improving the heavy industries.

The heavy industries produce farm and factory machinery. They also produce locomotives, railway cars, and trucks for new railways and roads. Shipyards are busy turning out new seagoing freighters. And transport by air is increasing. China is entering the modern age in transportation.

Coal is being mined in many parts of the country, and new oil fields are being developed. One of the most famous oil fields and refineries is far in the northwest in Taching. Along with the slogan, "In agriculture, learn from Tachai," there is another, "In industry, learn from Taching."

Children begin to learn these lessons almost as soon as they begin to talk.

9. School Days

Soon after sunrise on the cold mornings of north China's winter, children start for school. Before 7:30 A.M. they turn in at the schoolyard gates and make their way to their classrooms.

The morning session lasts from 7:30 to 11:15. After the noonday meal, the afternoon session usually runs from 1:30 to 3:00.

In winter children are dressed warmly. Boys and girls alike wear long padded pants and layers of padded cotton jackets. There are many quite cold "two-jacket days" and some very cold "three-jacket days."

The girls' jackets are brightly colored. Often girls wear bright hair ribbons, too. Pink is a favorite color for these. When the weather is warm, the girls wear skirts or bright cotton pants and blouses. Boys wear dark cotton pants and short-sleeved shirts. And they all wear sandals instead of warm boots.

When the children reach school in winter, they do not remove their outer jackets. They need all those layers of padding to keep warm in school, because classrooms are no warmer than the out-of-doors. The schools, like most buildings in China, have no central heat.

Kindergarten

Nearly half the children in China go to kindergarten at the age of four. Many of these children have already spent time in day nurseries. So they know how to play together nicely. They also know some little songs and dances.

In kindergarten, children learn to count, to read a few Chinese characters, and to sing and recite together. They dance and do exercises. They also hear stories and act out little plays that teach them devotion to their country and to its ways of life.

One little playlet that children seem to enjoy is about a child who finds a coin in the street. Instead of keeping it for herself, she hands it over to the traffic policeman at the corner.

In another playlet, a child has been given a basket of apples to pass around. He knows that he should give the bigger apples to the others and keep the smallest for himself. So he does. But one of the children says, "I am the smallest, so I should have the smallest apple."

Primary School

At the age of seven, Chinese boys and girls start five years of primary schooling. Instead of sitting at low tables on small chairs they can carry around easily, the primary school students sit at plain double wooden desks in long lines. Each desk has a bench wide enough for two. Most classes have 40 to 52 children.

When they are not reading or writing or doing arithmetic, the boys and girls sit quietly with their hands on the desks or folded behind their backs. When it is time for reading, though, the walls of the room almost shake with the sound! For the students all read aloud together at the tops of their voices.

In the writing periods, children learn the ABC's of the 26-letter Roman alphabet first. They write on their slates a simple word like *f-a-n*. In Chinese this means "food." Then the teacher draws on the blackboard the Chinese

A primary school classroom in Soochow. The children wearing red scarves are Little Red Soldiers.

character which stands for the word. She and the children draw the strokes with a finger in the air, until they have memorized the lines of the character. Finally they write it on their slates under the letters *f-a-n*.

For arithmetic the children use the abacus. An abacus is a frame in which beads can be moved along metal rods. A person who is skillful at flipping the beads of an abacus can figure sums as rapidly as with a calculating machine. Usually boys and girls start to use the abacus in the first year of primary school. By the third grade they can solve problems like $12 \div (3 \times 4) = ?$

Healthy bodies are considered as important as well-filled minds. So there are health classes to teach good eating and sleeping habits. School groups play games such as ping pong, volley ball, and basketball. And they do exercises. One set is for the eyes. Teachers say these exercises are one reason so few children wear glasses.

There is time in school for drawing. Usually the children all copy the same drawing. And they learn the old Chinese arts of folding paper into the forms of animals and of cutting colored papers into careful and beautiful designs.

Everyone learns to sing, and many children play musical instruments. The beat of the music is pounded out on plump red-sided drums, and various stringed instruments and horns carry the melody.

Songs and dances go together, and most of them are patriotic. They teach lessons about being good citizens of the People's Republic of China and about the joys of working for the commune and the state.

These songs and dances impress upon young people that all the 55 national minorities are truly part of the nation. Schools are teaching the 800 million people of China to live together pleasantly.

Boys and girls learn to work with their hands too. Many schools have vegetable gardens in which the students grow crops. And starting in kindergarten, classes spend an hour or two a week doing work for some factory.

Near one school there is a small factory where women make flashlight bulbs. Many of these women are mothers of children in the school. The finished bulbs are taken to the kindergarten. There the children fit the bases of the bulbs into holes punched on cardboard cards. They are really helping their mothers' work.

In another school seven-year-olds shape the firm bases for toothpaste tubes to be filled in a nearby factory.

A class of ten-year-olds makes ornamental lanterns of stiff colored cellophane. Some trace patterns on the sheets of cellophane. Others cut carefully along the lines marked by their classmates. The rest of the class fits together the cut pieces. The finished lanterns are then put into transparent sacks to be sold in a local department store.

Money from the sale of these products goes to the school. So the students are helping their school while they learn new skills.

Little Red Soldiers

As soon as children start primary school, they begin to think about joining the Little Red Soldiers. A boy or girl who wishes to join writes a letter. The teacher reads it to the class. The class discusses whether or not the child would make a good Little Red Soldier. By the fifth and last grade of primary school, 90 percent of the students belong and proudly wear their red neckerchiefs.

As serious students, Little Red Soldiers must spend one to two hours each day of the week except Sunday in an after-school study group. Anyone who becomes outstanding in some skill may be invited to attend a Children's Palace.

Children's Palaces

The liveliest after-school activities for boys and girls are offered in the Children's Palaces. Some Palaces occupy large houses that were once the homes of rich families. For others, buildings have been specially planned and constructed. There are many of these after-school centers in large towns and cities, but still there is not room for all the children who would like to spend time in them.

Each Palace has a management committee of twelve-year-olds. This committee helps decide which boys and girls shall attend.

In some rooms orchestras tootle and plunk and boom. In others dancers twirl and stretch. Boys and girls stand in line to play games that test their skill and strength. One can shoot toy guns at shapes of "enemy" war planes, or wriggle under barbed wire with a grenade in one hand, in these games. There are also stationary boats to row and bicycles to pedal.

Groups of young artists paint pictures, while other groups build airplane or ship models. There are classes in which soldiers teach the telegraphic code. Or one can learn to slide acupuncture needles under one's own skin at special spots. Twirling these needles properly can control pain and help sufferers from many ailments.

Coaches come to the Palaces to train young weight lifters, boxers, and boys who joust with long aluminum poles. Others help young athletes improve their tumbling and other acrobatic skills. There are teams practicing ice hockey, basketball, and other sports. The young people are as earnest about their play time as they are about their schoolwork.

Middle School

Five years of middle school follow the five primary years. Most students study a foreign language, which they may have started as early as third grade. English is the language most frequently chosen. French, German, Spanish, and Arabic are also popular. There are mathematics and science courses. And students may have a science lesson conducted in the foreign language they are studying.

Middle schools have changed in recent years. "Before the Cultural Revolution," a teacher explains, "the purpose of schooling was to prepare students for positions in the government or other professions. Young people were eager to find good positions and to get ahead in their careers. They stayed close to their books and had no feeling of kinship to the workers in factories and on farms. Now everyone is a worker in the Revolution. We substitute understanding and work experience for some of the old book knowledge."

Of the twelve months of the year, one month is spent in a factory, another month on a farming commune; 8½ months are spent in school and 1½ on vacation. Students in middle schools spend part of their school hours running the school bookshop, tending its garden, and doing practical factory work.

In one middle school, for example, some of the girl students sew for a clothing factory. They have a regular quota of factory work to turn out on their schoolroom sewing machines. A second group assembles small pieces of electrical equipment. A third group works in a foundry on the school grounds. There workers from outside come to help the teacher explain ways of molding metal.

Still other students are at work building new classrooms. The students on the school revolutionary committee decided in meetings with the teachers that they needed more space. They presented the project to the Education Bureau in their city and received the needed permit, money, and materials. Each student who works on the construction five or six days gets credit for part of his practical work experience.

The students have helped to plan the new building, as they help to plan their courses. At the start of construction, the boys dig ditches and the girls carry the earth away in baskets hung from shoulder yokes. So they learn to work together for the good of the community.

They learn new skills. And after each day's work they meet to praise good workers and to criticize any who have not done their share.

Work Experience

Most young people finish middle school at the age of seventeen. Then they are all assigned to some factory or farming commune for two years' work experience.

A girl from big-city Shanghai may be sent to work on a rubber plantation in the damp southwestern forests. A boy from the crowded lanes of Peking may be sent to a rural commune in a distant mountain region far from any town. Usually a small group from one school is assigned together, and a grown-up goes with them.

Boys and girls may not like the work they are assigned to do for those two years. They may not be happy to be sent far from home. They may not like the food. Or they may not get along well with some of the people under whom they work. But if they wish to live happily in the People's Republic, they must learn to accept and do whatever is asked of them.

A few are unhappy enough to run away from their assignments. Anyone who does this finds himself in a bad situation. Everyone has to show an identity card to travel, to get a job, or to buy foods like rice and sugar which are rationed. That identity card will betray a runaway. Such a person has no hope for the future unless he admits his error publicly. Then he must accept retraining in "right political thinking" about the Communist way of life. This training is usually combined with hard work in the fields.

Some students hope to go to a university or

A group of students prepares the soil for planting at an agricultural commune.

a teacher training institute or medical school, or possibly to train for a career on the stage. These young people must make a special effort to do well and show a willing spirit during those two years at work. For they must be recommended for further education by their coworkers. They will be judged largely on their "political understanding"—the value they place on doing whatever is asked of them for the state.

Not very many young people are chosen to go on to school. "You can use your knowledge and skills in a factory as well as in a university," those who are disappointed are told. "Street sweepers serve the Revolution as well as engineers."

People who are sent to rural communes in frontier areas are encouraged to settle there after their two years are over. Those who are sent to higher schools are encouraged to return to the community from which they were sent. The People's Republic of China is trying to train young people whose whole aim in life is to serve the state.

10. Holidays and Celebrations

Down the city street rumbles an open-backed truck. The back is crowded with young people. Horns blare. Drums boom. Voices call out in greeting from the truck. For these young people have been working far off in the country. They are home for the holiday. And they are ready to celebrate.

Workers in China do not have paid vacations. But they do have seven free days a year to celebrate the four official holidays. These are New Year's Day (January 1), May Day (May 1), National Day (October 1), and the Spring Festival at the beginning of the year according to the old moon calendar.

People have one day off for New Year's Day, and one for May Day. The anniversary of the founding of the People's Republic, the first of October, is celebrated for two days.

The first of June is international Children's Day. Parents do not all get a day off, since this is not one of the official holidays. But they try to visit the schools their children attend. For every school plans a special program of music and dances in colorful costumes for this day.

There used to be many feast days scattered through the old calendar. This was based on moon cycles rather than on the earth's circling of the sun. Most of those old holidays have been dropped by the Communist government as being too superstitious. The only feast of the old lunar or moon calendar that is still an official holiday is the Spring Festival. It marks the beginning of the lunar new year, which varies between late January and early February.

The Spring Festival accounts for three of the seven free days of the year. It is the favorite holiday in China, especially for family fun. School children are on their winter holiday at the time of the Spring Festival, so they are free to celebrate.

A city family may travel to visit relatives in

the old home town. Young people who are working far from home are given time off to visit their families. They come by bus or train or on open trucks.

There are many ways to enjoy a holiday. For the national days are celebrated all over the widespread country. And customs differ from one area to another.

Parades are generally popular. A parade may march through the banner-hung schoolyard of a rural commune. It may go down the village street of a tiny mountain hamlet where people used to dress in animal skins and huddle from the cold in birchbark shelters. It may pass in front of a grandstand where crowds of European businessmen and brightly dressed women used to gather for horse races in the "bitter past," when foreigners controlled most of China's cities. In those days Chinese were not welcome at the racecourse, but now it is a People's Park, and workers fill the stands. Or the parade may pause under the towering stone walls of one of the old Buddhist monasteries that once dominated the highland of Tibet.

In some areas red papers with lucky characters painted on them hang at doorways. Boughs of plum blossoms decorate some homes. Many

Schoolgirls assemble near Chairman Mao's statue to march in Shanghai's First of October parade.

small children are given bright balloons. And in every home there is certain to be a feast.

The table is covered with serving bowls and platters. There is scarcely room for the small plate and the rice or noodle bowl for each person. There is certainly plenty of food: whole fish, very tender under crisp brown skin, thin slices of duck meat, chicken, or shrimp with vegetables, steamed bread and dumplings, a big tureen of soup. For dessert there are fruits or some small sweet cakes. Bakeries and other shops usually stay open on the holidays for people with last-minute errands.

Holidays are meant for good times, and in China that means good food, family visits—and fireworks! Fireworks are an old Chinese invention. They splash marvelous colored patterns against the night sky over Chinese cities in honor of many events. They can be seen and enjoyed far and wide in the dark of night. But for daytime celebrations the most exciting place to be is Peking, the capital. And in Peking the place to be is Tien an Men Square.

Tien an Men means Gate of Heavenly Peace. The huge square is named for the gate at one end. This gate is really a large structure in the center of a long red wall. Five doorways in the gate lead into the grounds of the old Imperial Palace, long the home of China's emperors and their families.

In the days when emperors of the Ming and Ch'ing dynasties ruled China, no common person could pass through that gate. Whenever the emperor wanted to hand down a ruling or decree to the people, the message was placed in the beak of a golden phoenix bird. This bird figure was lowered from the top of the gate. There officials received the message from the golden beak and made it known to the people.

The gate came to symbolize the separation of the royal court from the people. So when the people began to rise up, a hundred years and more ago, it was before this gate that they gathered to protest against injustices.

When the Communists came to power, the palaces of the Forbidden City were opened to the people. The gate became a symbol of freedom. The Communists tore down buildings nearby to open a huge square. Along one side of the square they built the huge Hall of the National People's Congress. Across the way they opened two huge museums to honor the people's history. In the middle of the square, they erected a memorial to the war dead.

The square is paved with stone, all 98 acres of it. But on holidays scarcely a scrap of it can be seen. It is hidden by the great crowd of people. Almost a million people crowd into that square on some holidays!

Above their heads red banners float and bright balloons bob. At one end a space is kept clear for the great parade. It passes in front of the Gate of Heavenly Peace.

From the balcony above the gate, leaders of the People's Government review the marchers. These leaders do not represent an unseen and uncaring emperor. They represent the workers, peasants, and soldiers themselves.

The working people of China and their families gathered in that square and in many other parks and courtyards all lead simple, hardworking lives. Among them are sons and daughters of families that once were rich and powerful. Today no one in China is very rich. But the boys and girls of every family have equal opportunities for worry-free lives and for training to serve the state. That is what they celebrate as they cheer the parade on crowded Tien an Men Square.

Index

111

112

Meet the Author

Jane Werner Watson draws on personal experience in this book about the People's Republic of China. She is one of a small number of Americans who have had the opportunity to visit Communist China. To her China experience Mrs. Watson brought a familiarity with every country, except war-torn Laos and Vietnam, that borders China or the China Seas. She has traveled in the huge Soviet Union and all its satellites including Outer Mongolia; she has lived for several years in the crowded and troubled democracy of India; and she has observed Chinese cultural influences in the neighboring nations of Japan, Thailand, and tiny Bhutan, as well as Korea, Burma, Malaysia, Singapore, and the Philippines. This exposure to varied Oriental lands has enabled Jane Werner Watson to produce a perceptive book about the controversial world of the People's Republic of China.

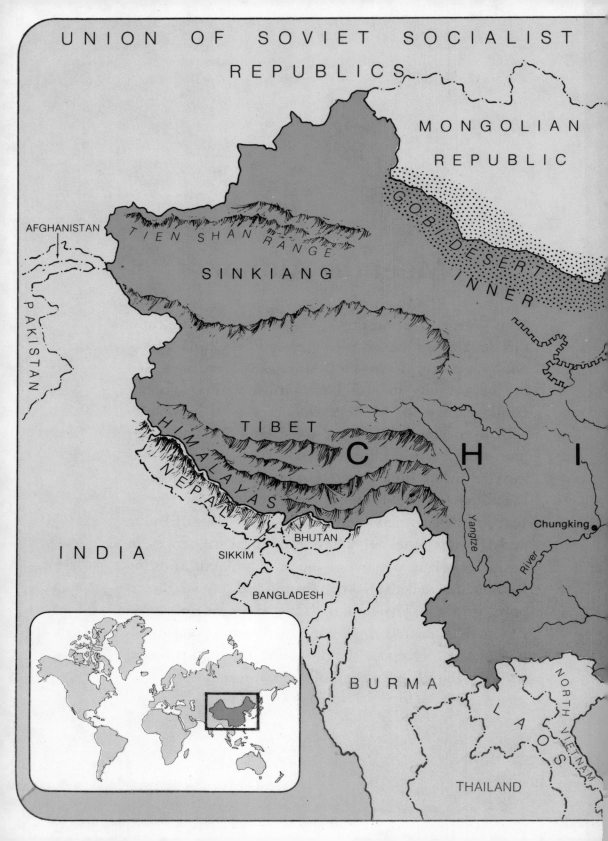